The ESS)f

CORPORATE TAXATION

Mark A. Segal, J.D., LL.M., CPA
Associate Professor of Accounting
University of South Alabama, Mobile, Alabama

Research and Education Association
61 Ethel Road West
Piscataway, New Jersey 08854

THE ESSENTIALS® OF CORPORATE TAXATION

Printed in the United States of America

Library of Congress Catalog Card Number 92-80488

International Standard Book Number 0-87891-892-2

ESSENTIALS is a registered trademark of
Research & Education Association, Piscataway, New Jersey 08854

WHAT "THE ESSENTIALS" WILL DO FOR YOU

This book is a review and study guide. It is comprehensive and it is concise.

It helps in preparing for exams, in doing homework, and remains a handy reference source at all times.

It condenses the vast amount of detail characteristic of the subject matter and summarizes the **essentials** of the field.

It will thus save hours of study and preparation time.

The book provides quick access to the important principles, theorems, concepts, formulas, and laws in the field.

Materials needed for exams can be reviewed in summary form – eliminating the need to read and re-read many pages of textbook and class notes. The summaries will even tend to bring detail to mind that had been previously read or noted.

This "ESSENTIALS" book has been prepared by an expert in the field, and has been carefully reviewed to assure accuracy and maximum usefulness.

Dr. Max Fogiel
Program Director

CONTENTS

CHAPTER 1

CORPORATIONS AND TAXATION

1.1   Sources of Tax Law

Sources of tax law include the Constitution, Internal Revenue Code, treaties, administration pronouncements, e.g., revenue rulings and revenue procedures, and judicial decisions.

1.2   Business Formats

There are a variety of types of business formats within which a business can be conducted. These include the sole proprietorship, partnership, regular corporation, "S" corporation, trust, and estate. In this book an examination of the major tax rules pertaining to corporations is made.

1.3   Corporate Characteristics

As a general rule a corporation formed in compliance with state law will be recognized for tax purposes. The tax law provides that there are six primary corporate characteristics. These characteristics are:

1)   Associates

1

2) An objective to carry on a business and divide the gains thereof

3) Continuity of life

4) Centralization on management

5) Limited liability

6) Free transferability of interest

1.3.1 Tax Treatment of Unincorporated Organizations

The tax law provides that an unincorporated organization will be treated as a corporation for tax purposes if it possesses more corporate characteristics than noncorporate characteristics, ignoring all characteristics common to both types of organizations.

1.3.2 Tax Treatment of Some Partnerships

In applying this rule a partnership will be subject to corporate taxation if it possesses more than three of the final four corporate characteristics listed. In contrast, a trust will be subject to corporate tax treatment if it possesses each of the first two corporate characteristics listed.

1.4 Major Tax Features of the Corporation

There are many aspects involved with corporate taxation.

1.4.1 Major Disadvantage of Corporations — Double Taxation

The regular "C" corporation is considered a taxpaying entity separate and apart from its shareholders. Frequently the regular corporate form is referred to as subject to double taxation. In this regard income is seen as taxed to the entity when earned by it, and to shareholders upon distribution. This aspect is generally seen as a drawback to use of a regular corporation. The regular corporation does however have a variety of other aspects which are beneficial.

1.4.2 Advantages of Corporations

The following are advantages of corporations:

1) Limited liability.

2) Enhanced means of raising capital through the issuance of debt or equity and the admission of new shareholders. In contrast the "S" corporation is permitted to have but one class of stock and a limited number and type of shareholders; while the partnership is generally viewed as terminated upon admission of a new partner.

3) Free transferability of interests.

4) Flexibility in selecting its taxable year.

5) Greater flexibility in the type and amount of retirement plans and tax free employee fringe benefits it can devise.

1.5 Procedural Elements

The due date of a regular corporation's tax return is the 15th day of the third month following the end of the corporation's tax year. Where the 15th day of such third month falls on a Saturday, Sunday, or legal holiday, the return due date is extended to the next business day thereafter. Filing is considered made when the return is mailed if sent by U.S. postage. The return must be filed with the I.R.S. Service Center that covers the district within which the corporation's principal business office or agency is situated. An automatic six month extension for filing can be obtained through the filing of a form 7004, and payment of any balance due for the return by the due date of the return for which the extension applies.

1.6 Tax Year

Regular corporations may select a calendar tax year or a fiscal tax year. A calendar tax year is one which begins on January 1 and ends on December 31. A fiscal tax year is one which begins on a date other than January 1 and ends on a date other than December 31. In contrast to regular corporations, personal service corporations and subchapter "S" corporations are subject to rules limiting their use of a fiscal tax year. A personal service corporation is a corporation characterized by having its primary activity being the providing of personal services by owner-employees. These services must be in the area of health, law, engineering, accounting, architecture, actuarial services, the performing arts, or consulting.

1.7   Tax Method

As a general rule due to recent changes in the tax law a regular corporation will typically be required to utilize the accrual method of accounting.

1.8   Structure of the Return

Determination of a corporation's tax is computed pursuant to the following steps:

(1) Gross Income from Operations — This consists of the total of:

Gross Profit from Goods or Services	Capital Gain Net Income
Dividends	Net Gain or Loss from Form 4797
Interest	Other Income
Gross Rents	
Gross Royalties	

(2) **Minus** Deductions — This category essentially consists of:

Compensation (less any jobs credit)	Depletion
Repairs	Advertising
Bad Debts	Contributions to Pension and Profit Sharing Plans

Rents	Allowable Costs of Employee Benefit Programs
Taxes	Other Deductions
Interest	Net Operating Loss
Charitable Contribution Deduction	Dividends Received Deduction
Depreciation	

(3) The difference between gross income and deductions equals the corporation's taxable income.

(4) Determine the tax liability by applying the pertinent tax rate schedule to the corporation's taxable income.

(5) Subtract from the tax the estimated taxes paid for the year, refunds to which the corporation is entitled that can be applied against the tax, and credits to determine the tax due or the amount to be credited against future taxes or to be currently refunded.

As reflected in the structure of the corporate tax above unlike individual taxpayers corporations lack:

1) An adjusted gross income figure;

2) A concept of itemized deductions and standard deduction amount; and

3) An exemption amount for regular tax purposes.

While in many other respects the determination of corporate taxable income and tax liability is analogous to that for individuals, as will become apparent several significant differences exist.

REVIEW QUESTIONS

1. *Name at least three types of different business formats.*

   Three different types of business formats are the sole proprietorship, partnership, and corporation.

2. *How many primary corporate tax characteristics are provided for in the tax law?*

   There are six primary corporate characteristics provided for in the tax law.

3. *What are the primary corporate tax characteristics?*

   The primary corporate tax characteristics are associates; an objective to carry on a business and divide the gains thereof; continuity of life; centralization of management; limited liability; and free transferability of interest.

4. *Under what circumstances may a partnership be treated as a corporation for tax purposes?*

   A partnership will be treated as a corporation for tax purposes if it has at least three of the following four characteristics: 1) continuity of life; 2) centralization of management; 3) limited liability; and 4) free transferability of interest.

5. *What is the corporate tax return form?*

   The corporate tax return form is the form 1120.

6. *When is the due date of the regular corporate tax return?*

   The regular due date of the corporate tax return form is the 15th day of the third month following the end of the corporation's taxable year, unless such 15th day falls on a Saturday, Sunday, or legal holiday in which case the return is due on the next business day thereafter.

7. *What are some differences between the tax return for individuals and that for corporations?*

The differences between an individual tax return and that for corporations include: an individual has a standard exemption amount, adjusted gross income, and exemption whereas a regular corporation does not for regular tax purposes.

CHAPTER 2

GAINS AND LOSSES UPON CORPORATE FORMATION

2.1   Formation

As a general rule taxpayers who exchange property for property must recognize a gain or loss on the transaction equal to the difference between the amount realized on the exchange and the basis of the property transferred. Internal Revenue Code (I.R.C.) Section 351 constitutes an exception to this treatment. As a general rule if a taxpayer transfers property solely for stock (stock or securities if the transaction occurred prior to October 3, 1989) and meets the criteria of Section 351 neither gain nor loss realized on the transaction will be recognized. Should the taxpayer however receive boot as part of an exchange otherwise satisfying Section 351 gain will be recognized to the extent of the lesser of the gain realized or the boot received.

2.2   Transfer of Property Upon Corporate Formation

Section 351 generally applies to transfers of property incident to formation of a corporation. Like other exchange nonrecognition provisions located in the tax law, Section 351 is premised upon the concept that the transaction produces no substantive change in the taxpayer's economic position; to qualify under Section 351 the following criteria must be met:

1) The transferor must receive stock for property. Securities received on the exchange will normally be viewed as boot. Property received by a transferor for the rendering of services is taxable to the transferor as compensation and ordinary income.

2) Immediately after the transfer the transferor (or transferors operating as a group) must be in control of the transferee corporation. Control exists for this purpose if the transferor(s) possess at least 80% of the total combined voting power of all classes of stock entitled to vote and 80% of any other shares of outstanding nonvoting stock.

2.2.1   Other Property Transfers

Taxpayers risk failure of the Section 351 requisites if transferring both services and property to the corporation for stock, should the services be substantial in value in comparison to the property transferred. In addition, qualification may be jeopardized if the transferor terminate(s) control either soon after the exchange or pursuant to a prearranged plan. Note that Section 351 can also apply to exchanges not related to the original formation of the corporation as well as those where the transferor possesses control of the corporation prior to the exchange so long as the Section 351 requisites are satisfied.

2.3   Gain or Loss on Section 351 Transactions

Section 351 is not an elective provision. If its elements are satisfied Section 351 will apply in determining the tax consequences of the transaction. Where Section 351 is strictly complied with and no boot is received, neither the corporation nor the transferor will recognize gain or loss realized. In addition, the shareholder will attain a basis in the stock received equal to that of the asset(s) transferred. The corporation meanwhile will obtain a basis in the property received equal to that of the transfer in the property. As a general rule the shareholder will be able to include the holding period of the property transferred in that of the stock received. The corporation will also be treated as having a holding period in the property received equal to that which the transferor had in such property.

Example:

John Brine transfers property in which he has a basis of $100,000 and which has a fair market value of $120,000 to Salt Sea Corporation in return for 100% of its stock. Since this constitutes a Section 351 transaction in which no boot was received, the $20,000 gain realized on the transaction will not be recognized by either John or the corporation. John will acquire a $100,000 basis in the stock received, and the corporation a $100,000 basis in the property received from John.

2.4   Impact of Boot on Recognition

Where the transferor receives boot from the corporation in a transaction otherwise qualifying under Section 351, gain realized will be recognized to the extent of the lesser of the gain or boot received. Boot is property other than stock. The corporation would not however be subject to tax on a Section 351 transaction.

Example:

Mickey Dee transfers property with a basis of $75,000 and a fair market value of of $150,000 to Zeon Corporation for stock valued at $130,000 and $20,000 in cash. Mickey has a gain realized of $75,000 on the transaction ($150,000 amount realized minus $75,000 basis). Of this gain $20,000 must be recognized as this is the lesser of the gain realized and the boot received. The character of the gain depends upon the nature of the asset in the hands of the transferor. The corporation however would not be subject to tax.

2.5   Impact of Boot on Basis

The computation of basis for shareholder in stock received in a Section 351 transaction is computed pursuant to the following steps:

	Basis in the property transferred
Minus	Boot Received
Plus	Gain Recognized

Thus, in the previous example, Mickey's basis would be $75,000 ($75,000 minus $20,000 boot received plus $20,000 gain recognized). The transferor's basis in any boot received is equal to the fair market value of the boot on the date of receipt. Where the transaction produces a loss since the transferor recognizes no gain or loss, the transferor's basis equals the basis of the property transferred less the boot received.

In contrast to the computation of basis to the transferor, the corporation (transferee) obtains a basis in the property it receives equal to the basis of such property in the hands of the transferor plus any gain recognized by the transferor. In the previous example, the corporation would obtain a basis in the property received equal to $95,000 ($75,000 plus $20,000 gain recognized by the transferor).

2.6   The Nature of Stock

Stock is generally considered a capital asset, the sale or exchange of which produces a capital gain or loss. Whether the capital gain or loss will be characterized as long term or short is dependent on the shareholder's holding period in the stock. The holding period of stock acquired in a Section 351 exchange includes the holding period of the asset transferred to receive it. In contrast the holding period of boot received in a Section 351 exchange begins on the date of receipt.

Where stock becomes worthless in the hands of the shareholder, the shareholder will realize a capital loss equal to the basis in the stock. In determining if the loss upon worthlessness is long term or short term the stock is considered to have become worthless on the last day of the taxpayer's taxable year in which worthlessness occurs.

Example:

J transfers some raw land which has been held for investment for a six month period to a corporation in return for stock representing a 90% interest in the corporation. In addition, on the exchange J receives an automobile. The holding period of the stock received includes the holding period of the raw land held, but the holding period of the automobile begins on the date of receipt.

2.7   Special Rules Regarding Liabilities

As a general rule the assumption of a liability by a transferee corporation in a transaction otherwise qualifying under Section 351 will not be treated as boot for purposes of recognition of gain but will be taken into account in determining the transferor's basis in the stock received.

A liability will be treated as boot for recognition of gain purposes in the following situations:

1) The principal purpose of transferring the liability was to avoid federal income taxes, or

2) The transfer of the liability lacked a bona fide business purpose.

Example:

G transfers property with a basis of $50,000 and subject to a liability of $10,000 in return for 85% of the stock of Z corporation. The liability was taken out by G immediately before the exchange and lacked a bona fide business purpose. The stock received on the exchange has a value of $75,000. G will have to treat the $10,000 liability relief as boot and will have a gain recognized on the exchange of $10,000.

2.8   Liabilities in Excess of Basis

Where liabilities assumed by the transferee corporation exceed the basis of the property transferred, as a general rule, the excess liability relief will be treated as boot and gain recognized to the transferor. The transferor's basis in the stock received in such instance will normally be zero. The transferee corporation in such event will normally have no recognized gain and will attain a basis in the asset received equal to the basis of the asset in the hands of the transferor plus any gain recognized by the transferor as a result of the transaction.

Example:

Z, an individual, transfers property with a basis of $25,000 and subject to a $30,000 liability to a corporation in exchange for 90% of the corporation's stock. As a result of this transaction Z will have a $5,000 gain recognized ($30,000 liability relief minus $25,000 basis) and obtain a basis of zero in the stock received ($25,000 basis minus $30,000 liability relief plus $5,000 gain recognized).

2.9   Capital Considerations

To raise capital the corporation faces many alternatives. The most prominent of these alternatives concerns whether to utilize debt or issue equity to raise capital. Debt is often preferred by corporations as it enables the payment of tax deductible interest whereas the payment of dividends on stock are not deductible.

Another factor to consider is what type of stock to issue for tax purposes. While stock generally constitutes a capital asset the sale or exchange of which produces a capital gain or loss, exceptions to this characterization exist. For example through the issuance of stock qualifying as Section 1244 stock (small business corporation stock) the shareholder may be allowed to treat a loss on the disposition of the stock as an ordinary loss. While treatment as small business corporation stock is advantageous, in contrast stock of a collapsible corporation is not. As a general rule gain on the sale of stock in a collapsible corporation is treated as ordinary income.

A collapsible corporation is a corporation formed or availed of principally to manufacture, construct, or produce property; or buy Section 341 assets or hold stock in such a corporation. Section 341 assets for this purpose are assets held for less than three years which give rise to ordinary income upon disposition.

13

REVIEW QUESTIONS

1. *What is Internal Revenue Code (I.R.C.) Section 351?*

   Internal Revenue Code Section 351 is an Internal Revenue Code provision that has particular relevance to corporate formations. If the criteria of Section 351 are satisfied, no gain or loss will be recognized on the transfer of property to a corporation solely for stock.

2. *What are the Section 351 criteria?*

   In order for a transaction to be subject to Section 351:

   a) The party (parties) transferring property to the corporation must receive solely stock on the exchange.

   b) Immediately after the transfer of property for stock the transferor(s) must have control of the corporation.

3. *Is subjection to Section 351 elective?*

   No, subjection to I.R.C. Section 351 is mandatory if the Section 351 criteria are satisfied.

4. *Will gain or loss be recognized on a Section 351 transaction if boot is received?*

   If boot is received gain will generally be recognized to the extent of the lesser of the boot received or the gain realized. No loss however will be recognized on a Section 351 transaction even if boot is received.

5. *Will liability relief be considered boot for purposes of gain recognition under Section 351?*

   Generally liability relief will not be considered boot received for purposes of gain under Section 351. Exceptions to this treatment exist however. One such exception requires that gain be recognized on a Section 351 transaction at least to the extent liability relief exceeds the basis of property transferred to the corporation.

14

6. *J transfers property with a basis of $50,000 and a fair market value of $75,000 for 90% of the outstanding stock of a corporation and $5,000 in cash. What is the basis and gain recognized to J and the corporation as a result of the exchange?*

As a result J will have to recognize $5,000 as this is the lesser of the gain realized and boot received. J will obtain a basis in the stock received of $50,000 ($50,000 basis transferred minus $5,000 boot received plus $5,000 gain recognized). The corporation will not be considered to have any gain recognized on the transaction and will obtain a basis of $55,000 in the property received ($50,000 basis of the transferor plus the gain recognized by the transferor on the exchange).

CHAPTER 3

TAX RULES UNIQUE TO CORPORATIONS

3.1   Special Tax Rules

Certain unique tax rules distinguish the computation of a corporation's tax liability from that of other taxpayers. Unique rules in this regard pertain to the treatment of capital gains and losses, depreciation recapture, net operating losses, charitable contributions, organizational expenses, and the treatment of dividends received.

3.2   Capital Gains and Losses

Much like an individual taxpayer a corporate taxpayer must net capital gains and losses on an annual basis. The actual treatment of such gains and losses however is markedly different from that accorded individuals. These differences include:

1) Unlike individual taxpayers for whom the maximum tax rate on capital gains is lower than that for ordinary income, the net capital gain of corporate taxpayers is subject to the same tax rate as ordinary income.

2) While individuals can utilize at least some portion of capital losses in excess of capital gains as a deduction against

ordinary income, corporations are only permitted to use capital losses to offset capital gains.

3) While individuals can carryforward excess capital losses an unlimited number of years, corporations are required to carryback excess capital losses three years and if any capital losses remain, carryforward the excess for a period of five tax years.

3.3   Depreciation Recapture

Much like individuals in determining the characterization of gain upon the taxable sale or exchange of depreciable Section 1231 property held for more than one year, corporations are subject to the depreciation recapture rules of Sections 1239, 1245, and 1250.

Section 1231 property includes several different types of property, the most significant of which are the following if held long term:

1) Depreciable personal property used in a trade or business

2) Real estate used in a trade or business

3) Property held to produce rental income

4) Leaseholds held for more than one year

5) Capital assets which have been involuntarily converted

6) Business property held for more than one year which has been subject to a theft or casualty

In addition, however, corporations may be subject to a special recapture provision — that recapture provision being I.R.C. Section 291. According to Section 291 where the corporation sells an asset subject to Section 1250 recapture 20% of the excess that would have been recaptured had Section 1245 instead applied must also be recaptured.

In general the depreciation recapture provisions of these sections operate as follows:

1) I.R.C. Section 1239 requires that recognition of gain on the sale of depreciable property between related parties to be treated as ordinary income.

2) I.R.C. Section 1245 requires that the lesser of the gain to be recognized or the depreciation taken be recaptured and treated as ordinary income. Section 1245 applies to depreciable personal property, e.g., equipment and machinery, and to depreciable nonresidential real estate that is depreciated under an accelerated method of depreciation.

3) Section 1250 generally requires that the lesser of the gain to be recognized or the depreciation taken in excess of that which would have been taken under the straight line method be recaptured and treated as ordinary income. Section 1250 applies to depreciable residential real estate, e.g., an apartment building, and depreciable non-residential real estate depreciated under the straight line method.

Example:

Neon Corporation has an apartment building which it bought several years ago, and in which it has an adjusted basis of $40,000 and has taken a total of $20,000 in depreciation. Had straight line depreciation been utilized $10,000 in depreciation would have been taken. Neon sells the building for $70,000. Neon's gain on the sale is $30,000. Of this gain $10,000 is considered ordinary income under Section 1250 (as this is the lesser of the excess of accelerated depreciation over straight line or gain realized).

In addition, since Neon is a corporation, it must recapture an additional $2,000 under I.R.C. Section 291. This results because this amount is 20% of the additional amount that would have to be recaptured had Section 1245 applied to the transaction. Note that under Section 1245 an additional $10,000 would have been recaptured as this is the lesser of $10,000 remaining depreciation taken (in excess of that already recaptured under Section 1250) and $20,000 remaining amount of gain to be recognized.

3.4   Net Operating Loss

A net operating loss is essentially the amount by which the corporation's business expenses exceed its business income. In contrast to the computation of net operating loss by individual taxpayers no adjustment of taxable income to determine net operating loss is needed for personal exemptions or nonbusiness deductions.

A net operating loss can be used to offset taxable income and is subject to a three year carryback and a 15 year carryforward. However, one can elect out of a carryforward. An election out must be made by the due date (including extensions) of the return for the year in which the net operating loss arose. An election out may be desirable where the taxpayer expects to be in a higher tax rate in future years and thus expects to derive a greater tax savings by increasing the amount of net operating losses useable in future years.

3.5   Charitable Contributions

A corporation can take a charitable contribution deduction for a tax year limited to the lesser of the amount of the contribution(s) or 10% of the corporation's taxable income computed without regard to the charitable contribution deduction, any net operating loss carrybacks, or dividends received deduction. Contributions made in excess of the limit may be carried forward for a five year period.

3.6   Special Rules Regarding Contributions

The amount of the charitable contribution deduction attributable to property is:

1) Generally the fair market value of long-term capital gain property.

2) The lesser of the fair market value or basis of short-term capital gain or ordinary income property.

3) Basis plus one-half of any appreciation for certain research property and ordinary income property useable toward the exempt purpose of the charitable organization.

In addition, it should be noted that accrual basis corporations are permitted to include in the computation of their current charitable contribution deductions an amount authorized by their board of directors to be donated to charity by the end of the taxable year, which is donated by the 15th day of the third month following the end of the taxable year.

Example:

In 1992, Z Corporation donated land held for investment to the First Baptist Church. The land had been purchased in 1989 for $50,000 and had a fair market value of $80,000 at the time of the contribution. The corporation is considered to have made a charitable contribution for tax purposes of the full fair market value of the property ($80,000).

The actual amount of the $80,000 deductible in a year may be subject to a limitation such as that limiting the charitable contribution deductions of corporations to 10% of their adjusted taxable income.

3.7   Dividends Received Deduction

In order to mitigate the potential for triple taxation, corporations are permitted a dividends received deduction for the dividends received from other domestic corporations. As a general rule the dividends received deduction is the applicable deduction percentage multiplied by the lesser of the corporation's taxable income or the dividends received. Should the applicable percentage multiplied by the dividends received however produce a net operating loss, the dividends received multiplied by the applicable percentage will equal the dividends received deduction. As reflected in the table below the applicable percentage depends upon the percentage of stock held by the corporate shareholder in the distributing corporation.

Percentage Ownership	Applicable %
Less than 20%	70%
At least 20% but less than 80%	80%
80% or more	100%

Example:

B Corporation owns a 25% stock interest in Z Corporation. During the year Z distributes a $50,000 dividend to B. Excluding the dividend B has $60,000 of gross income and $30,000 in deductions. Based upon these facts the dividends received deduction is 80% of $50,000 or $40,000 as this is the lesser of 80% of the dividends received or 80% of taxable income before the dividends received deduction.

3.8   Organizational Expenses

Expenses incurred to organize the corporation (not including costs to transfer property by the corporation or print and sell stock or securities) are permitted to be amortized over a 60 month period. In order to amortize these expenses an appropriate election must be made for the corporation's first taxable year. In computing amortization the amortization period begins on the date the corporation begins business.

Failure to make the election will result in the organization having to capitalize its organizational costs. Any organizational costs not written off by the time the corporation terminates its business can be deducted in the year of such termination.

REVIEW QUESTIONS

1. *How do corporations differ from individuals with regard to the treatment of capital losses?*

   Individuals can apply at least a portion of capital losses in excess of capital gains against ordinary income. In the case of most individuals this amount is limited to $3,000 ($1,500 in the case of taxpayers who are married filing separately). Any excess capital losses which cannot be used due to tax limitations can then be carried forward for an unlimited period and retain their status as capital losses. Corporations, in contrast, can only utilize capital losses to offset capital gains, with any excess capital losses having to be carried back a period of three years and forward for a period of five years.

2. *Determine the amount and character of gain recognized by the corporation in the following situation: B Corporation acquires an apartment building for $100,000 in 1986. It depreciates the building under an accelerated method taking some $50,000 in depreciation on it at which time it sells the building for $90,000. Had straight line depreciation instead been taken the depreciation over the same period would have been $30,000.*

   As a result of the sale B Corporation has a gain realized and recognized of $40,000. This gain equals $90,000 amount realized on the sale minus $50,000 adjusted basis in the building. Of this gain some $22,000 is characterized as ordinary income due to recapture and $18,000 is Section 1231 gain. The amount recaptured is equal to the excess of the depreciation taken in excess of that taken under the straight line method $20,000 ($50,000 minus $30,000) under the circumstances and $4,000 (which is 20% of the lesser of the $20,000 gain to be recognized and the $30,000 remaining depreciation taken).

3. *What is net operating loss?*

   A net operating loss is generally the amount by which business expenses exceed business income.

22

4. *How is a net operating loss utilized?*

A net operating loss is used to offset taxable income. Rather than give rise to a current refund for the current year's return due to production of a negative income figure for the current taxable year the net operating loss is subject to a three year carryback and a 15 year carryforward. Taxpayers can elect out of the carryback period if they so desire however.

5. *What is the limit on a corporation's charitable contribution deduction for a taxable year?*

A corporation is limited to deducting charitable contributions up to a figure of 10% of the corporation's taxable income before the net operating loss or dividends received deduction.

6. *When can a corporation's charitable contribution deduction for a year include an amount not already contributed to charity?*

This can occur when the corporation has been authorized to make a contribution by its board of directors before the end of the taxable year and in fact makes such a contribution before the 15th day of the third month following the end of the taxable year.

7. *J Corporation has $50,000 of gross income before taking into account any dividends received. During the year it received $50,000 in dividends from a domestic corporation in which it had a 5% interest and incurred some $60,000 in operating expenses. What is J Corporation's dividends received deduction for the taxable year?*

J Corporation can take a dividends received deduction of 70% of the lesser of the $50,000 dividends received or 70% of its taxable income before the dividends received deduction (as 70% of the dividends received would not produce a net operating loss). Thus, J Corporation will have a dividends received deduction of $28,000 (70% multiplied by $40,000).

8. *Over what period can organizational expenses be amortized?*

   Organizational expenses can be amortized over a 60 month period.

9. *What must a corporation do to qualify to amortize its organizational expenses?*

   In order to amortize its organizational expenses a corporation must elect to amortize such expenses on its first tax return for the year it begins business.

10. *What is the tax consequence if the corporation does not elect to amortize such expenses?*

    If the corporation does not elect to amortize such expenses the corporation must capitalize such expenses, and can only write off such expenses in the period it terminates business.

CHAPTER 4

TAX LIABILITY ARISING FROM CORPORATE DISTRIBUTIONS

4.1 Corporate Distributions

Distributions made by an ongoing corporation to its shareholders are considered a dividend to the extent the distribution is deemed paid out of earnings and profits (E and P). Any amount distributed in excess of the E and P attributed to the distribution is considered a return of capital, going first toward recovery of the shareholder's stock basis with any excess being treated as a capital gain.

There exist two types of earnings and profits accounts. These are current earnings and profits and accumulated earnings and profits. Current earnings and profits are those earnings and profits that arose during the taxable year in which the given distribution was made. Accumulated earnings and profits meanwhile is the balance of earnings and profits at the inception of the current taxable year.

4.2 Computation of E and P

E and P is similar but not exactly the same as retained earnings and profits. As a general rule E and P is increased by all items of income, whether or not taxable (except for gains realized but not recognized on an involuntary conversion). Likewise, it is generally reduced for expenses paid whether or not deductible.

In determining the character of distributions made by an ongoing corporation to its shareholders the following rules are applied in allocating E and P.

1) Allocate current E and P to each of the distributions made during the period. Allocation to a particular distribution is made pursuant to the following formula:

$$\text{Current E\& P} \times \left(\frac{\text{Amount of Distribution}}{\text{Total Amount Distributed during the Years}} \right)$$

If the amount distributed during the year is less than the amount of current E and P the entire amount distributed is treated as a dividend, and reportable by the shareholder(s) as ordinary income.

Should the total amount distributed exceed the balance of the current E and P, then the balance of the accumulated E and P must be examined. Any positive balance is then allocated to the distributions made during the year, beginning with the earliest such distributions to characterize such distributions to the extent not covered by an allocation of current E and P.

Example:

Byron Corporation has $10,000 of current earnings and profits and $12,000 of accumulated earnings and profits. During the year Byron makes five distributions of $5,000 each to its shareholders. Of the total $25,000 that has been distributed some $22,000 will be considered a dividend, and $3,000 a return of capital. An allocation of the respective accounts reveals that $2,000 of the current earnings and profits will be allocated to each distribution made during the year ($10,000 multiplied by [5,000 divided by 25,000]). Three thousand of the $12,000 accumulated earnings and profits will be allocated to each of the first four distributions. Thus, whichever shareholders receive the first four distributions will report receipts from

26

these distributions as entirely ordinary income dividend. The recipient of the final distribution will have a dividend of $2,000 and a $3,000 return of capital.

2) Should current E and P be positive and accumulated E and P be negative, in characterizing distributions to shareholders accumulated E and P is ignored and current E and P is allocated as described in (1).

3) Should both current and accumulated E and P be negative, any distribution will be characterized as a return of capital.

4) Should current E and P be negative and accumulated E and P be positive, the tax law requires that the positive balance of accumulated E and P be offset by some portion of current E and P to determine the positive balance of E and P for each date a distribution is made.

4.3   Effect of Asset Distributions

Cash — If cash is distributed the amount distributed is simply the amount of cash distributed. The corporation will recognize neither gain nor loss on the distribution, but will decrease its earnings and profits as of the end of the year by the amount distributed.

Property — The fair market value of property distributed is the amount considered distributed to the shareholder. Unlike a cash distribution a corporation will recognize a gain on the distribution of property to a shareholder to the extent the fair market value of the asset distributed exceeds the corporation's basis in it. Should the fair market value of the asset distributed be less than the basis of such asset, the tax law does not permit a loss to be recognized and deducted. Where a gain is recognized upon a distribution the corporation's earnings and profits are increased by the gain recognized and decreased by the fair market value of the asset distributed.

Property subject to a liability — If a corporation distributes property with regard to which the shareholder takes on responsibility for a liability the corporation will be deemed to have made a distribution equal to the greater of the fair market value of the asset distributed or the liability relief obtained. The shareholder who receives such a distribution will obtain a basis in the asset equal to the greater of the fair market value of the asset or the liability assumed or taken subject to. The amount of the distribution considered received by the shareholder for purposes of determining any inclusion in gross income resulting from the distribution will however be the fair market value of the asset reduced by the liability taken.

4.4   Constructive Dividends

In some instances when a corporation provides a benefit to a shareholder, e.g., a below market interest rate loan or an inflated salary, the Service may challenge the benefit as a constructive distribution by the corporation despite there being no formal declaration of a distribution. In determining the characterization of such distribution the earnings and profits must be allocated to the amount involved in much the same manner as it would in the case of a formal distribution.

4.5   Distributions in Other Forms

In addition to the traditional distribution of property or cash, corporations may also engage in other types of distributions.

4.5.1   Stock Dividends

Stock dividends are not taxable if proportionate. Basis in nontaxable stock dividend received is equal to:

Basis multiplied by the (FMV stock dividend divided by the FMV of the stock on which the dividend was received plus the FMV of the stock dividend).

A stock dividend will be taxable however where:

1)   The shareholder has the option to take stock or property as the distribution.

2)   Some shareholders receive stock and some receive other

28

types of property (thus, altering the shareholders proportionate interest in the corporation).

3) Distributions of convertible preferred stock, unless it is established not to be a disproportionate distribution.

4) Distributions of preferred stock to some common shareholders and the receipt of common stock by some shareholders.

5) Distributions of property to certain shareholders and distributions to other shareholders resulting in an alteration of their interest in the assets or earnings and profits of the corporation.

Should the distributions be taxable, the shareholders will acquire a basis in the stock received equal to the FMV of such stock on the date of distribution.

4.5.2   Stock Rights

Stock rights are generally not taxable. If not proportionate, however, or falling into one of the exceptions similar to those for stock dividends, a distribution will be taxable, and the shareholder will acquire a basis in the stock rights equal to the fair market value of such rights on the date of distribution.

If not taxable, basis need not be allocated to the stock rights if their value does not exceed 15% of the FMV of the stock on which the rights were distributed. However, if the shareholder desires to allocate part of his basis to nontaxable stock rights with a value not exceeding 15% of the fair market value (FMV) of the stock on which the distribution is made he may elect to do so. In allocating basis to nontaxable stock rights a procedure similar to that in allocating basis to a nontaxable stock dividend is utilized. This is evident in the following formula which is used to make such allocation.

Basis of stock on which rights are received multiplied by the (fair market value of stock rights divided by the sum of the FMV of the rights and the FMV of the stock on which the rights were received).

The application of this formula is reflected in the following example.

X owns 100 shares of M Corporation in which he has a $15,000 basis. X receives 100 nontaxable stock rights worth $1,000 in a nontaxable distribution. At the time of the distribution the stock on which the rights are distributed have a value of $20 per share. Since the value of the rights received are less than 15% of the value of the stock on which they were distributed, X need not allocate any of the basis in his stock to the stock rights. If X desires to make an allocation of basis to the stock rights, he may do so pursuant to an election. Should X make such an election he will obtain a basis in the stock rights of $714 ($15,000 basis in stock multiplied by $1,000 the value of the stock rights divided by $21,000 the sum of the value of the rights and the value of the stock on which the rights were received on the date of distribution). In addition the election will cause the basis of the stock to be adjusted to $14,286 ($15,000 the basis to be allocated multiplied by $20,000 divided by $21,000 which is the sum of the value of the stock and the stock rights on the date of distribution).

REVIEW QUESTIONS

1. *What is the relevance of earnings and profits to the treatment of distributions made by an ongoing corporation?*

   Distributions made by an ongoing corporation to its shareholders are considered a dividend and ordinary income to the extent covered by earnings and profits allocated to the distribution.

2. *What are the types of earnings and profits accounts?*

   There are two types of earnings and profits accounts. These are current earnings and profits and accumulated earnings and profits.

3. *How is the amount of property distributed determined?*

   The amount of property distributed is generally considered to be the fair market value of such property.

4. *What are the tax consequences to a shareholder of receiving a distribution of property subject to a liability?*

   The amount considered received where property is distributed subject to a liability for purposes of determining inclusions in income is equal to the fair market value of the property minus the amount of the liability. The basis of the property received however is generally equal to the fair market value of the property received without reduction for any liability attached to it.

5. *What is a constructive dividend?*

   A constructive dividend exists where a corporation provides a benefit to its shareholder for less than adequate consideration to the extent the excess benefit is covered by earnings and profits. Unlike the traditional dividend distribution a constructive dividend is not a formally declared distribution. A common example of a constructive dividend is where a shareholder gets paid an inflated salary for doing nominal work for the corporation, and the corporation has substantial earnings and profits.

6. *Bill received a nontaxable distribution of 1,000 shares of common stock on 1,000 shares already held in the corporation. The value of the stock received was $10 a share on the date of distribution. Bill possessed a basis of $5,000 in the shares already held which was the value of such stock. What is Bill's basis in the shares received as a stock dividend?*

Bill's basis in the shares received as a stock dividend is $3,333. This amount equals $5,000 multiplied by (10,000 divided by 15,000).

CHAPTER 5

THE TAXABILITY OF VARIOUS REDEMPTIONS

5.1   Redemptions

A redemption involves a corporation's acquisition of its stock in exchange for property or cash. If the redemption meets certain criteria it will be treated as a sale or exchange of the shareholder's stock to the corporation. Such a sale or exchange will result in gain or loss recognized to the extent of the difference between the shareholder's amount realized from the corporation and the shareholder's adjusted basis in the stock transferred. In contrast should the redemption not qualify for sale or exchange treatment, the amount received from the corporation will be treated as a distribution from an ongoing corporation and characterized as dividend to the extent covered by the corporation's earnings and profits. Thus, sale or exchange treatment is generally preferable to shareholders than regular distribution treatment as basis is recovered tax free, and a tax will only apply should there be a gain. Any gain recognized from such sale or exchange will normally be characterized as capital gain and be able to absorb capital loss; whereas, otherwise the entire amount distributed risks being taxed as a dividend.

5.2   Types of Redemptions

There are three principal types of redemptions eligible for sale or exchange treatment. These types are:

1) Redemptions not essentially equivalent to a dividend (I.R.C. Section 302(b)(1)).

2) Redemptions substantially disproportionate with respect to the shareholder (I.R.C. Section 302(b)(2)).

3) Redemptions in complete termination of the shareholder's interest (I.R.C. Section 302(b)(3)).

4) Redemptions made to noncorporate shareholders in complete liquidation (I.R.C. Section 302(b)(4)).

5) Redemptions made in order to pay death taxes (I.R.C. Section 303).

5.3   Attribution

The rules enabling qualification for sale or exchange treatment generally require that there be an actual and significant reduction in the shareholder's stock interest in the corporation for there to be sale or exchange treatment. In determining if a sufficient decrease exists the shareholder's interest in the corporation both before and after redemption are examined based upon the stock held directly and indirectly by the shareholder.

Stock not held directly by the shareholder will be attributed to a shareholder in the following circumstances:

1) If held by the shareholder's spouse, children, grandchildren, and parents.

2) Proportionate interest in the corporation held by partnerships, estates, and trusts in which the shareholder has an interest.

3) Proportionate in a corporation in which the shareholder has at least a 50% interest.

4) An option to buy stock is treated as stock owned for purposes of these rules.

Some limit is placed on attribution in that: (a) stock attributed to a family member from within group (1) above cannot be attributed to the shareholder, and (b) stock will not be attributed from the shareholder of an entity to another party.

5.3.1 Section 302(b)(1)

This is the most vague and least reliable of the possible means of qualifying for sale or exchange treatment. Generally at the very least to qualify under this provision the shareholder must lose control. Pursuant to the actual provision there must be a meaningful reduction of interest.

5.3.2 Section 302(b)(2)

Section 302(b)(2) provides a mechanical test to determine if one sale or exchange treatment qualifies. This test contains two elements:

1) After the distribution the shareholder must own less than 80% of the proportionate interest of the outstanding stock and less than 80% of the proportionate interest in the common stock held prior to the distribution.

2) After the distribution the shareholder must have less than 50% of the outstanding combined voting power of all classes of stock entitled to vote in the entity.

Example:

X, Y, and Z own 50, 100, and 50 shares, respectively, of Brie Corporation. The stock held by X, Y, and Z constitute 100% of the outstanding stock of Brie. Y redeems 20 shares for $20,000 in cash. Y had purchased the shares for $5,000 some five years previously. As a result of the redemption Y has 80 of what are now 180 shares outstanding of Brie. While this percentage is less than 50%, it fails to qualify for sale or exchange treatment under I.R.C. Section 302(b)(2) as his interest has fallen from 50% to 44.44% which is not less than 80% of Y's previously held interest in the corporation. In order to satisfy the 80% standard, Y would have had to redeem at least 34 shares of Brie Corporation.

5.3.3 Section 302(b)(3)

This Section enables sale or exchange qualification if the shareholder's interest is completely terminated. Should a taxpayer terminate holding a direct interest in the corporation, qualification may still be prevented by attribution of the stock held by another to the taxpayer. The tax law however allows a waiver of such attribution if certain criteria are met and an appropriate agreement is filed with the IRS. This agreement essentially provides that the taxpayer will not acquire an equity interest in the corporation for a ten year period (absent possible acquisition as an heir or as a creditor). In addition, the taxpayer must not become an officer or director of the corporation within the ten year period.

5.3.4 Section 302(b)(4)

Unlike the other Section 302 provisions qualification under Section 302(b)(4) is determined based upon examination of the impact of the distribution on the corporation rather than the change in the interest held in the entity by the taxpayer. To qualify for a sale or exchange under this provision:

1) The distribution must be pursuant to a plan to terminate an active trade or business which was not acquired in a nontaxable transaction.

2) The distribution is of a trade or business not acquired in a taxable transaction occurring during the five year period preceding distribution.

3) Execution of the plan to liquidate that portion of the business will be completed by the end of the next year.

4) The distribution reflects a genuine contraction of the business.

5) The corporation prior to the distribution had at least two trades or businesses in existence for at least five years.

5.3.5   Section 303

This provision allows for sale or exchange treatment with regard to redemptions meeting certain criteria up to a maximum amount of the death taxes resulting from the decedent's death plus the amount of funeral and administration expenses deductible by the estate. Section 303 only applies to stock in a closely held business with regard to which the value of the stock exceeds 35% of the decedent's adjusted gross estate. The adjusted gross estate equals the decedent's gross estate minus estate deductions. In determining if the 35% standard is satisfied, the stock of two closely held businesses can be aggregated should the decedent have at least a 20% interest in each.

5.3.6   Related Corporations

Where shareholders redeem stock in one corporation by selling it to another corporation in which the shareholder has control the transfer will generally be viewed as a redemption by the corporation whose stock was transferred.

5.4   Preferred Stock Bailout

As a general rule, if a shareholder receives preferred stock in a nontaxable distribution at a time when the corporation has earnings and profits, such stock will be considered tainted and give rise to ordinary income when sold at a gain to the extent of the earnings and profits attributable to the distribution. Should the later sale of the preferred stock produce a loss, however, no loss will be recognized. When the preferred stock is later redeemed by the corporation, amounts received will be treated as dividend income to the extent of the corporation's earnings and profits on the date of redemption. Note certain exceptions to the above treatment exist, the most significant of these exceptions concern situations where the shareholder sells all of his stock interest in the corporation to an unrelated party.

REVIEW QUESTIONS

1. *What is a redemption?*

   A redemption consists of a corporation's acquisition of its stock in return for cash or other property.

2. *Does a corporation recognize gain or loss on a redemption of its own stock?*

   A corporation will not recognize either a gain or a loss as a result of a redemption of it's own stock.

3. *What is the effect to a shareholder of a stock redemption?*

   A shareholder will either treat amounts received in a redemption of the shares held in the redeeming corporation as a regular corporate distribution (dividend to the extent of earnings and profits and the excess as a return of capital) or as an amount realized on a sale or exchange of stock.

4. *Which treatment of a redemption is preferable from a shareholder's perspective?*

   Generally, sale or exchange treatment is preferable to the shareholder. This results because if sale or exchange treatment applies the shareholder can recover an amount up to basis in the stock redeemed tax free, and should the amount exceed basis the excess will receive capital gain treatment. In contrast, where a redemption is treated as a regular distribution dividend treatment will result to the extent the distribution is covered by earnings and profits.

5. *What are the different types of redemptions qualifying for sale or exchange treatment?*

   The major types of redemptions qualifying for sale or exchange treatment are those satisfying the criteria of either Internal Revenue Code Sections 302(b)(1), 302(b)(2), 302(b)(3), 302(b)(4), 302(g), or 303.

6. *What type of redemption is particularly relevant with regard to death taxes?*

   The redemption provision of Internal Revenue Code Section 303 is particularly directed to abet satisfaction of death taxes and related costs.

CHAPTER 6

THE TAX TREATMENT OF CORPORATE LIQUIDATIONS

6.1   Liquidating Distributions

Different tax treatment applies to distributions made by a corporation undergoing liquidation than to a corporation that remains an ongoing entity. Liquidation for this purpose is a process undergone by the corporation in order to cease being an ongoing concern.

A corporation will generally recognize gain or loss upon distributing an asset in a liquidating distribution. The amount of such gain or loss is measured by the difference between the fair market value of the asset distributed and the adjusted basis of the asset in the hands of the corporation. Should the fair market value of the asset be greater than its adjusted basis a gain will result. Should, however, it be less, a loss will be produced. Characterization of any gain or loss produced upon a liquidating distribution is dependent upon the nature of the asset in the hands of the distributing corporation.

Where the liquidating corporation distributes property and the shareholder takes the property subject to a liability or assumes a liability, the corporation is treated as having made a distribution equal to the greater of the fair market value of the property distributed or the liability relief obtained.

6.2   Limitations on Loss Recognition

The following rules limit the ability of corporations to recognize losses realized upon the distribution of property in a liquidating distribution:

1) Upon distribution to a shareholder with a more than 50% interest in the corporation (determined by aggregating the interest held directly and that held indirectly) where the property has been contributed to the corporation with a built in loss and either:

a) the distribution is not pro rata, or

b) the property distributed is disqualified property.

Disqualified property includes:

1) Property acquired by the corporation in an I.R.C. Section 351 exchange.

2) Property acquired by the corporation as a contribution to capital within five years before the date of distribution.

3) Property acquired through a transaction engaged in by the corporation with regard to which the basis is determined by reference to disqualified property falling in category (1) or (2) above.

An additional rule limits recognition of loss to prevent a corporation from circumventing the nonrecognition of loss rules by selling assets for fair market value following adoption of a plan of liquidation, recognizing the loss, and then distributing the proceeds to its shareholders. According to this exception where the asset was contributed to the corporation in a Section 351 transaction in which the principal purpose was recognition of loss, then the basis of the asset must be reduced but not below zero to the fair market value of the asset on the date of contribution.

Example:

John owns 70% and his wife Mary 30% of Sunrise, Inc. John contributes property to Sunrise in which he has a basis of $75,000 and which has a fair market value of $60,000. Two years later in carrying out a liquidation, Sunrise distributes the property to John. At the time of the distribution the property has a fair market value of $55,000. The built-in loss of $15,000 cannot be recognized by the corporation. The additional $5,000 loss attributable to the decrease in the asset's value following its contribution to the corporation however can be recognized by the corporation. Had the property's value instead been $65,000 at the time of the distribution none of the loss realized could be recognized.

A special rule applies without regard to the percentage interest held in the corporation by a shareholder with regard to built-in losses. According to this rule, where property with a built-in loss is contributed to a corporation, and the principal purpose of such contribution is recognition of a loss upon liquidation, the adjusted basis of the property must be reduced by the built-in loss in computing loss upon distribution. This rule is generally not applicable when the corporation holds the asset for more than two years before distribution.

6.3   Treatment of Shareholders

Shareholders who receive liquidating distributions must generally recognize gain or loss based upon the difference between the adjusted basis of their stock and the fair market value of the asset received. A gain will exist if the fair market value of the property plus any cash received on the liquidating distribution exceeds the shareholder's adjusted basis in the corporate stock. A loss will however result if the amount realized (cash plus fair market value of other property received) is less than the shareholder's stock basis. As the property considered transferred by the shareholder for the amount received is considered stock any gain or loss by the shareholder attributable to a liquidation distribution will be generally considered capital gain or loss.

If the property received is subject to a liability which the shareholder assumes responsibility for, the amount realized on the distribution is reduced by the amount of the liability.

The shareholder's basis in any property received in a liquidation is generally equal to the fair market value of such property even if the property is distributed with a liability.

6.4   Liquidation of Subsidiaries

A parent-subsidiary relationship exists when one corporation owns at least an 80% interest in the other. The 80% interest must exist with regard to both the combined voting power and the total value of the subsidiary stock. If a parent-subsidiary relationship exists on the date of liquidation no gain or loss will be recognized upon a distribution made by the subsidiary to the parent and certain corporate tax attributes, e.g., basis, carryovers, and net operating losses, of the subsidiary will carry over to the parent.

To qualify for the above treatment all liquidating distributions must be made within one year of adoption of a formal plan of liquidation.

6.5   Minority Shareholders

The regular rules regarding recognition of gain or loss apply to a liquidating distribution made by a subsidiary to a minority shareholder.

REVIEW QUESTIONS

1. *What is a liquidation?*

   A liquidation is the process undergone by a corporation in order to discontinue the corporation's business operations.

2. *What are the tax consequences to a corporation of undergoing a liquidating distribution of property?*

   A corporation will generally recognize a gain or loss upon making a liquidating distribution of property to a shareholder. Such gain or loss will be measured by the difference between the fair market value of the asset distributed and the basis the corporation has in such asset. If the fair market value is greater than basis, a gain will be produced. If the fair market value is less than basis, a loss will result. The character of such gain or loss is dependent upon the nature of the asset distributed.

3. *What are the tax consequences to a shareholder receiving a liquidating distribution from a corporation?*

   Generally a shareholder who receives a liquidating distribution will recognize a gain or loss as a result of the receipt of a liquidating distribution. The amount realized by a shareholder on such distribution is generally equal to the amount of cash plus fair market value of other property received. Any such gain or loss will generally be a capital gain or loss to the shareholder as it is considered to result from the disposition of the shareholder's stock in the corporation.

4. *Do exceptions to the recognition of gain or loss by a corporation on the distribution of property as a liquidating distribution exist?*

   Exceptions exist to the ability of a corporation to recognize a loss in certain situations involving a liquidating distribution. These exceptions are meant to prevent the abusive manufacturing of losses by corporations and shareholders.

CHAPTER 7

TAX TREATMENT FOR CORPORATE REORGANIZATIONS

7.1   Corporate Reorganizations

Through the undergoing of a corporate reorganization it is possible to acquire relief from recognition of gain or loss that would otherwise have to be recognized on a sale or exchange of property. Gain however will have to be recognized in certain instances where boot is received on a corporate reorganization but not a loss.

As a general rule, a corporate reorganization entails the transfer of substantially all assets or stock in a corporation in a transaction that meets the following requirements and satisfies one of the types of reorganizations listed in Internal Revenue Code Section 368.

1) Continuity of Proprietary Interest — Shareholders of the target corporation receive stock in the acquiring corporation. Generally the stock should be voting stock. The target corporation for this purpose is that corporation transferring substantially all of its assets or control.

2) Continuity of Business Enterprise — A significant portion of the target corporation's business must be continued or a significant portion of its assets used in business operations of the acquiring corporation.

3) Bona Fide Business Purpose — There must exist a valid non-tax business purpose for undergoing the reorganization.

4) Plan — There should be a plan of reorganization. Note however that the regulations do not make the presence of a written plan mandatory to qualify as a reorganization.

7.2 Type "A" Reorganization

The "A" reorganization is the most flexible type of reorganization in that up to 50% of the consideration provided by the acquiring corporation can be other than voting stock. There exist two types of "A" reorganizations.

Merger — One company absorbs another.

Consolidation — Two or more corporations combine to form a new corporation.

Other aspects of the "A" reorganization:

1) Generally a majority (usually at least two-thirds) of the shareholders of each entity must approve.

2) The acquiring corporation must generally assume responsibility for all of the liabilities of the target corporation.

7.2.1 Tax Ramifications of the "A" Reorganization

Generally as part of the "A" reorganization, the target corporation immediately distributes stock or assets received to its shareholders in return for their stock in the target corporation. Should only stock be received in the acquiring or new corporation, no gain or loss will be recognized. Should property other than such stock be received by a shareholder, then any gain realized will be recognized to the extent of the lesser of the gain realized or boot received.

Acquiring Corporation — The acquiring or new corporation of an "A" reorganization will not recognize gain or loss as a result of the reorganization and will acquire a basis in the assets received equal to those in the hands of the transferor increased by any gain recognized by the transferor.

7.3   Type "B" Reorganization

To qualify as a "B" reorganization the acquiring corporation is required to use solely voting stock to garner control of the target corporation. Control is defined for this purpose as the possession of at least 80% of the combined voting power of each class of stock and 80% of each class of nonvoting stock. Rather than acquire the target's assets, the acquiring corporation in a "B" reorganization acquires control of the target corporation by acquiring stock from shareholders of the target. The shareholders who transfer their shares in the target corporation solely for voting stock will have no recognized gain or loss as a result of the exchange and will acquire a basis in the acquiring corporation stock received equal to the basis that they had in the target corporation stock transferred.

7.4   Type "C" Reorganization

Pursuant to a "C" reorganization substantially all of the assets of the target corporation are acquired for voting stock. The consideration allowable in a "C" reorganization is more flexible than that permitted in a "B" reorganization. At least 20% of the target's assets can be acquired for boot. In determining if appropriate consideration has been transferred, liabilities assumed by the acquiring corporation are ignored unless other boot consideration is provided.

To qualify as a "C" reorganization the target corporation must distribute all stock and assets received from the acquiring corporation as well as any other properties not transferred (in accordance with the plan of reorganization). While generally no gain or loss is recognized by the target corporation (absent distribution of appreciated property not received in the reorganization), the target's shareholders may have a recognized gain upon distribution from the target to the extent of the lesser of the boot received or gain realized. In determining the holding period of stock received in the acquiring corporation the target's shareholders may generally tack their holding period in the old stock to that in the stock received.

7.4.1 Effect of Boot on Basis

As in the case of a like kind exchange where boot is received, the target corporation shareholders will acquire a basis in the stock received equal to their basis in the stock transferred minus boot received plus gain recognized.

The acquiring corporation will acquire a basis in the assets received equal to the basis of such assets in the hands of the target corporation increased by any gain recognized by the target.

7.5 Type "D" Reorganization

The "D" reorganization may well have the most complicated type of the reorganization provisions. In contrast to most other types of reorganizations, it is typically engaged in to divide the corporation. There exist three types of "D" reorganizations. These are the spin-off, split-off, and the split-up.

7.5.1 Spin-Off

The spin-off involves a corporation transferring one of its businesses to a new corporation in an I.R.C. Section 351 transaction and promptly distributing stock received in the new corporation to its shareholders. Thus, resulting in the shareholders of the parent corporation acquiring stock in both the original and the resulting corporations.

7.5.2 Split-Off

The split-off is similar to the spin-off except that the original shareholders transfer all or some of their shares back to the original corporation in return for stock or securities in the new corporation.

7.5.3 Split-Up

In the split-up two new corporations are formed by the original corporation. This is followed by the distribution of the stock in the new corporation in return for the stock held by the shareholders in the original corporation. Thus, as a result the original shareholders acquire stock in the two resulting corporations and the original corporation goes out of existence.

7.5.4 Exceptions

Usually a "D" reorganization will not produce a gain or loss. Nevertheless one should be cautious of the following special rules:

1) Should securities be received as part of the reorganization, the principal amount of which exceeds the principal amount of the securities surrendered a tax will be imposed on up to the excess fair market value of the securities received.

2) The transaction will be taxable if it is principally a device to distribute earnings and profits of the transferor or transferee.

3) Where boot other than stock or securities is received dividend or gain treatment may result.

7.6   Type "E" Reorganization

The "E" reorganization is commonly referred to as a recapitalization. Unlike the other types of reorganization thus far discussed the "E" reorganization involves but one corporation. Essentially the "E" reorganization entails a corporation changing its capital structure. Generally pursuant to an "E" reorganization no gain or loss is recognized upon a creditor converting bonds for stock or the exchange of common or preferred stock between shareholders.

7.7   Type "F" Reorganization

An "F" reorganization involves the mere change in identity, form, or place of the organization. A common example of an "F" reorganization is the changing of the entity's state of incorporation or the changing of the entity's name. No change in basis to either the corporation or its shareholders takes place in an "F" reorganization, and the resulting corporation assumes the tax attributes that existed previously.

7.8 Type "G" Reorganization

The "G" reorganization was established in the Bankruptcy Tax Act of 1980. To be a "G" reorganization, certain requisites must be satisfied. Among these requisites is that the corporation must be in foreclosure, receivership, or a similar proceeding under state law or Chapter X of the Federal Bankruptcy Law. Pursuant to a "G" reorganization, control of the corporation must be transferred to creditors of the debtor corporation.

REVIEW QUESTIONS

1. *What happens to the capital loss carryovers and net operating losses of a target corporation in a corporate reorganization?*

   These are generally assumed by the acquiring corporation.

2. *What is the rationale behind the nonrecognition of gain or loss on a corporate reorganization?*

   The nonrecognition of gain or loss possible in the case of a corporate reorganization is rooted in the concept of continuity of investment. In essence it is believed that the shareholders of the target corporation have not undergone a substantive change in their economic position. Similar logic is noticeable in other nonrecognition provisions such as the like kind exchange provisions of Section 1031.

3. *X Corporation acquires 90% of the total outstanding stock of Y Corporation from the shareholders of Y solely in exchange for voting stock. Does this qualify as a reorganization and if so what type of reorganization is it?*

   This fact pattern would seem to qualify as a reorganization. In fact it would be a "B" reorganization.

4. *F Corporation has two businesses in which it has been actively engaged for seven years. F transfers the assets of one of the businesses to a newly formed corporation in return for all of the stock of the newly formed corporation. F then proceeds to distribute the shares received in the new corporation to its shareholders. What type of reorganization if any has been engaged in?*

   This scenario would qualify as a "D" reorganization. It would in fact be a spin-off.

5. *As part of a reorganization the shareholders of the target corporation receive stock with a fair market value of $50,000 and cash*

of $10,000 in return for stock in which they have a basis of $45,000. What is the amount of gain realized and recognized on the transaction by the shareholders?

As a result the shareholders would have a $15,000 gain realized ($60,000 amount realized minus $45,000 basis), and $10,000 gain recognized (as this is the lesser of the gain realized and the boot received).

6. *Will a loss realized on a reorganization be recognized?*

No, a loss realized on a corporate reorganization cannot be recognized.

7. *What is the continuity of proprietary interest test with regard to corporate reorganizations?*

The continuity of proprietary interest is a judicial doctrine which requires that shareholders of the target corporation of a corporate reorganization retain some prescribed equity interest in the acquiring or resulting corporation in order for the transaction to qualify as a reorganization. Satisfaction of this rule is one of the major differences distinguishing a reorganization from a taxable sale or exchange and is linked to the notion that the transaction should not be taxable as it involves no substantive change in economic position.

CHAPTER 8

PENALTY TAXES

8.1 The Two Penalty Taxes

To motivate corporations to distribute their earnings two special additional tax provisions exist. These are the accumulated earnings tax and the personal holding company tax. These taxes are nondeductible and mutually exclusive.

8.2 Accumulated Earnings Tax

The accumulated earnings tax is based upon the corporation's accumulation of earnings beyond its reasonable needs. In order to be held liable for this tax the corporation must generally have been formed or availed of in order to avoid income tax by shareholders on amounts otherwise receivable.

8.2.1 Reasonable Business Needs

Since the accumulated earnings tax is premised upon the accumulation of earnings in excess of reasonable business needs it is important to determine what constitute reasonable business needs. Reasonable business needs include such items as reserves for liability, redemptions, expansion of the business, and working capital needs.

8.2.2   Working Capital

In determining the working capital needs of the corporation courts have focused upon the corporation's operating cycle. A commonly accepted method used to determine a corporation's working capital needs is the Bardahl formula.

According to the Bardahl formula working capital needs are determined by adding the inventory and receivables turnover of the corporation and subtracting from this sum the accounts payable turnover. The result is then converted to a percentage for the year which is multiplied by the company's cost of goods sold and other expenses (not including depreciation and tax expenses).

Example:

Midas Corporation has an inventory turnover of 50 days, a receivable turnover of 75 days, and a payable turnover of 60 days. Assuming Midas has a combined cost of goods sold and other allowable operating expenses of $600,000 its working capital needs under the Bardahl formula amount to $108,333. This amount is determined by multiplying 600,000 by 18.05556%. This percentage is used as it equals the sum of the receivable and inventory turnover in days minus the payable turnover in number of days multiplied by 360.

8.2.3   Taxation of Excess Earnings

A 28% tax rate applies to excess accumulated taxable income. This tax is imposed in addition to the tax the taxpayer would otherwise owe. Even should excess accumulated earnings exist, the accumulated earnings tax can be largely, if not entirely, avoided due to the existence of an accumulated earnings tax credit [(an exemption) of the greater of $250,000 ($150,000 for personal service corporations) or the demonstrated reasonable needs of the business].

8.2.4   Accumulated Earnings Tax Dividends Paid Deduction

In addition, to the accumulated earnings tax credit, subjection to an accumulated earnings tax can be further diminished by a deduction for accumulated earnings tax purposes of dividends:

1) Paid during the year.

2) Taxable to shareholders as ordinary income and distributed within two-and-one-half months after the end of the taxable year.

3) Amounts which the shareholder agrees to be taxed upon although not actually distributed.

8.2.5 Steps in the Computation of Accumulated Earnings Tax

Follow these steps:

	Taxable Income
Plus	Dividends Received Deduction
Plus	Capital Loss Carryovers and Carrybacks
Plus	Net Operating Loss Deduction
Minus	Corporate Income Tax
Minus	Capital Loss in excess of Capital Gain
Minus	Charitable Contributions in excess of 10% limit
Minus	Dividends Paid or Deemed Paid
Minus	Net Long-Term Capital Gains over Short-Term Capital Loss
Minus	Accumulated Earnings Credit
	Accumulated Earnings Taxable Income

If subject to the accumulated earnings tax the tax is computed by multiplying the applicable accumulated earnings tax rate by accumulated taxable income.

8.3 Personal Holding Company Tax

A personal holding company is subject to a 28% flat tax rate on undistributed personal holding company income. This tax is imposed in addition to the corporation's regular tax. A personal holding company is a corporation controlled by five or fewer individuals during the last half of the corporation's taxable year and produces what is predominantly investment type income. In determining if five or fewer individuals possess such interest stock attribution rules are applicable.

8.3.1   Excluded Corporations

The tax law excludes certain corporations from possible subjection to personal holding company tax. Major types of corporations so excluded include: foreign personal holding companies, small investment companies, tax exempt organizations (under I.R.C. Section 501(a)), insurance companies, and banks.

8.3.2   Income Test

In addition to the stock ownership test at least 60% of a corporation's adjusted ordinary gross income must be from passive personal holding company income. Adjusted ordinary gross income for this purpose is defined as gross income minus short-term capital gain, long-term capital gain, Section 1231 gain, and rent and royalties reduced by certain expenses.

Personal holding company income is defined as interest, rents, royalties, and dividends. If more than 50% of the corporation's adjusted ordinary income is derived from adjusted rents or adjusted royalties then rents and royalties will be considered personal holding company income.

8.3.3   Computation of Personal Holding Company Tax

If subject to the personal holding company tax a flat tax rate of 28% is imposed on personal holding company taxable income. Personal holding taxable income is determined pursuant to the following computation.

	Taxable Income
Plus	Dividends Received Deduction
Plus	Net Operating Loss (other than for previous taxable years)
Plus	Business Expenses and depreciation on non-business property in excess of income received on such property
Minus	Regular corporate income taxes accruable
Minus	Charitable Contributions Deduction above the 10% limit up to the limit on individuals
Minus	Net Capital Gain after Taxes
	Adjusted Taxable Income
Minus	Dividends Paid Deduction
	Undistributed Personal Holding Company Income

8.3.4 Personal Holding Company Dividends Paid Deduction

As in the case of the accumulated earnings tax vulnerability to the personal holding tax can be mitigated by the payment of dividends during the taxable year or within two-and-one-half months after the end of the taxable year in much the same manner as applies to the accumulated earnings tax.

REVIEW QUESTIONS

1. *What are permissible reasons to accumulate earnings?*

   Acceptable reasons to accumulate earnings include: the need to expand the business, the need to acquire plant or equipment, and the need to satisfy legitimate legal obligations such as lawsuits.

2. *What is the amount of the accumulated earnings tax credit?*

   The accumulated earnings tax credit is generally $250,000 ($150,000 in the case of personal service corporations) unless a valid business reason can be shown to justify a greater accumulation, in which case more can be accumulated.

3. *What are the taxes on excess accumulated earnings and personal holding company income?*

   The taxes on excess accumulated earnings and personal holding company income are penalty taxes which must be paid in addition to the taxes that would otherwise be due. At present the tax rate for this type of tax is 28%.

4. *Are the accumulated earnings tax and the personal holding tax mutually exclusive?*

   Yes.

5. *How do dividends paid or deemed paid affect the computation of personal holding company tax?*

   The amount of such dividends has the effect of reducing the amount of personal holding company tax that would otherwise be owed as it reduces the amount of taxable income upon which the tax is based.

6. *In order for the accumulated earnings tax to apply, the corporation must have been formed for a proscribed "bad purpose." What is meant by this?*

A bad purpose exists if the corporation has been formed or availed of in order to avoid income being taxed to the shareholders. This purpose need not be the dominant purpose. The presence of this purpose will generally be assumed to exist if the corporation accumulates income beyond its reasonable business needs.

7. *What is a personal holding company?*

A personal holding company exists for tax purposes if:

a) The corporation has more than 50% of the value of the outstanding stock owned by five or fewer individuals at some point during the last half of the taxable year.

b) At least 60% of the corporation's adjusted ordinary gross income is composed of passive type income.

8. *In determining whether the stock ownership percentage test is met are attribution rules applicable?*

Stock attribution rules are applicable in determining if a corporation is a personal holding company.

CHAPTER 9

ALTERNATIVE MINIMUM TAX

9.1   Alternative Minimum Tax

The alternative minimum tax for corporations operates in much the same manner as the alternative minimum tax does for individuals. The primary purpose of the alternative minimum tax is to assure that taxpayers with a substantial amount of economic wealth (income) do not avoid paying their fair share of taxes.

Form 4626 is utilized to compute the alternative minimum tax for corporations. As reflected on the form, the alternative minimum tax owed for a given taxable year is equal to the amount by which the corporation's tentative minimum tax exceeds the corporation's regular tax liability for the year.

9.2   Steps in the Computation

In determining a corporation's alternative minimum tax the following steps are utilized:

	Taxable Income (before the net operating loss deduction)
Plus	Tax Preferences
Plus or Minus	Tax Adjustments
	Alternative Minimum Taxable Income (AMTI) before Net Operating Loss Deduction and Adjusted Current Earnings Adjustment
	Alternative Minimum Taxable Income before Net Operating Loss Deduction and Adjusted Current Earnings Adjustment
Plus or Minus	Adjusted Current Earnings Adjustment
	Alternative Minimum Taxable Income before Net Operating Loss Deduction Minus Alternative Minimum Tax and Net Operating Loss Deduction
Minus	Alternative Minimum Tax Exemption Amount
	Alternative Minimum Tax Base multiplied by 20%
	Alternative Minimum Tax before Foreign Credit
Minus	Foreign Credit (Subject to a possible 90% limitation)
	Tentative Minimum Tax Minus Regular Tax Liability
Minus	Regular Tax Liability
	Alternative Minimum Tax

9.3   Preference Items

An alternative minimum tax preference item can only function to increase the amount of alternative minimum taxable income. Major preference items include:

1) Accelerated depreciation taken in excess of straight line (for assets placed in service before 1987).

2) Tax exempt interest on state and local bonds, the funds of which are not applied for an essential function of the government.

3) Charitable contribution deductions for the donation of property, where the charitable contribution deduction exceeds the basis of the property.

4) Intangible drilling costs to the extent exceeding 65% of the net income from the properties.

5) Amounts related to certain amortizable pollution control facilities.

6) Percentage depletion claimed in excess of the adjusted basis of property.

9.4   Adjustments

Adjustments can produce an increase or decrease in alternative minimum taxable income. Major types of adjustments pertain to:

1) Amortization of certain pollution control facilities placed in service after 1986.

2) Depreciation of tangible property placed into service after 1986.

3) Basis adjustments for determining gain or loss on the sale or exchange of property.

4) Post-February 28, 1986 long-term capital gains.

5) Passive activities of certain personal service corporations and closely held corporations.

9.5   Adjusted Current Earnings (ACE)

The ACE adjustment is a new adjustment for taxable years beginning after December 31, 1989. The Adjusted Current Earnings adjustment can result in an increase or decrease of alternative minimum taxable income.

Alternative Minimum Taxable Income will be increased by 75% of the amount by which Adjusted Current Earnings exceeds Alternative Minimum Taxable Income before Net Operating Loss or the Adjusted Current Earnings adjustment. Should Adjusted Current Earnings be less than the Alternative Minimum Taxable Income before the Net Operating Loss or Adjusted Current Earnings adjustment, Alternative Minimum Taxable Income will be reduced by 75% of the difference.

Adjusted Current Earnings are computed by taking the Alternative Minimum Taxable Income before the Net Operating Loss or Adjusted Current Earnings adjustment and making certain prescribed adjustments.

9.6   Exemption Amount

The regular exemption amount for corporate Alternative Minimum Tax purposes is $40,000. This amount is decreased by 25% of the excess of the corporation's Alternative Minimum Taxable Income in excess of $150,000. Thus, the exemption will be completely phased out should the corporation have Alternative Minimum Taxable Income of at least $310,000.

9.7   Alternative Minimum Tax Rate

The Corporate Alternative Minimum Tax rate is a flat 20%.

9.8 Foreign Tax Credit

Within limits Alternative Minimum Tax can be offset by a foreign tax credit (generally a maximum of 90% of the foreign tax credit can be used); and general business credits including the investment tax credit carryover can be used subject to a limit of 25% of Alternative Minimum Tax liability.

9.9 Minimum Tax Credit

The tax law permits the Alternative Minimum Tax paid in one year to be carried forward and used to offset the taxpayer's regular tax liability should the tax liability exceed the tentative minimum tax.

REVIEW QUESTIONS

1. *What is the purpose of the Alternative Minimum Tax provisions?*

    The purpose of the Alternative Minimum Tax is to make certain that taxpayers who make a substantial amount of economic income do not avoid paying their equitable share of taxes.

2. *How do adjustments differ from preferences for Alternative Minimum Tax purposes?*

    An adjustment may result in an increase or decrease in the Alternative Minimum Taxable income. In contrast, an Alternative Minimum Tax preference only acts to increase Alternative Minimum Taxable income.

3. *What form is filed by a corporation for Alternative Minimum Tax purposes?*

    The form used by corporations for Alternative Minimum Tax purposes is Form 4626.

4. *What is the tax rate for corporate Alternative Minimum Tax?*

    The tax rate applicable to corporations for Alternative Minimum Tax purposes is 20%.

5. *A corporation has Alternative Minimum Taxable income of $250,000. What is the corporation's Alternative Minimum Tax exemption amount?*

    The corporation's exemption amount under these circumstances is $15,000 ($40,000 tentative exemption amount less 25% of the $250,000 Alternative Minimum Taxable income less $150,000).

6. *How does the Alternative Minimum Tax relate to a taxpayer's regular tax?*

    The Alternative Minimum Tax is owed if the taxpayer's tentative minimum tax exceeds the taxpayer's regular tax. If such excess exists, the taxpayer's Alternative Minimum Tax is generally equal to the difference and is paid in addition to the taxpayer's regular tax.

CHAPTER 10

CONTROLLED CORPORATIONS

10.1 Types of Controlled Corporations

Special rules apply to a group of controlled corporations. There exist two principal types of controlled groups. These are the parent-subsidiary group and the brother-sister group.

10.2 Parent-Subsidiary Corporation Relationships

A parent-subsidiary group exists where one corporation (the common parent) possesses at least 80% of the total combined voting power of all classes of stock entitled to vote or at least 80% of the total value of all classes of stock in more than one corporation. Note that a parent-subsidiary relationship will exist should one corporation have at least 80% of the total value of all voting stock or at least 80% of the total value of all classes of stock.

10.3 Brother-Sister Corporation Relationships

A brother-sister controlled group exists if five or fewer individuals, trusts, or estates own at least 80% of the value of two or more corporations, with the aggregate common ownership of the identified shareholders exceeding 50% of the voting power or value of the corporation's shares.

In determining the amount of common ownership in two corporations held by an individual where the individual holds stock in two corporations the lesser of the percentage of shares held in the corporations by the individuals, trusts, or estates is used.

10.4   Section 338

Pursuant to Internal Revenue Code Section 338 should at least 80% of the voting power and 80% or more of the value of all classes of stock (except for nonvoting, nonparticipating preferred stock) be acquired by purchase from an unrelated party during a 12 month period an election may be made to treat the target corporation as having sold all of its assets for their full fair market value as of the day the 80% standard is met. To be effective the election must be irrevocable and made by the 15th day of the ninth month following acquisition of the necessary percentage.

In determining the amount realized and basis to be allocated to the respective assets of the acquired corporation, a particular formula is prescribed. The amount deemed realized is to be allocated according to a prescribed hierarchy.

Gain or loss will result should the amount allocated to an asset differ from the asset's basis in the hands of the acquired corporation. The character of any gain or loss resulting is dependent upon the nature to which the gain or loss relates.

10.5   Satisfaction of Subsidiary Debt

Where a subsidiary satisfies a debt to its parent corporation through the transfer of property the fair market value of which exceeds its adjusted basis the subsidiary is generally required to recognize gain realized on the transaction. No gain however will be recognized by the subsidiary if it is undergoing a liquidation pursuant to Internal Revenue Code Section 332. I.R.C. Section 332 mandatorily applies if a parent corporation liquidates a subsidiary and the following requisites are met:

1) The parent owns at least 80% of the outstanding voting stock of the subsidiary and at least 80% of the total value of all classes of stock.

2) The subsidiary distributes all property in complete liquidation of its stock within the tax year or within three taxable years from the year in which a plan of liquidation is adopted and the first distribution is made.

3) The subsidiary is solvent.

10.6   Section 482

To minimize the potential shifting of income and the manufacturing of losses, Internal Revenue Code Section 482 authorizes the Service to reallocate items of income, deduction, and credit to prevent the avoidance or evasion of tax or to more clearly reflect income.

10.7   Consolidated Returns

In certain cases a parent-subsidiary controlled group is permitted to file a consolidated return. Filing a consolidated return is not mandatory. In order to file a consolidated return it is necessary that each member of the controlled group consent to the filing of a consolidated return. Once a consolidated return is filed the controlled group is required to continue to file such type return until it otherwise obtains the consent of the Internal Revenue Service to revoke the election.

10.7.1   Effect of a Consolidated Return

A consolidated return has the effect of treating the controlled group of corporations as a single corporation for tax reporting purposes. As a result, intercompany transactions generally offset one another and net operating losses produced by one member of the controlled group can be used to reduce the taxable income of the group as a whole. Net operating losses produced by a member of the group in a tax year before consolidation can typically only be used to offset income of the corporation producing the loss.

10.8   Taxation of Related Corporations

In computing the tax of related corporations the corporations are treated as one corporation. Thus, each of the related corporations is entitled to only have their pro rata share of the income within the lower tax rate ranges subject to such lower tax rate. For example, if there are three related corporations and the first $50,000 of a corporation's taxable income is subject to a 15% tax rate, then only $16,667 of each of the three corporations taxable income may be subject to such lower tax rate (one-third of $50,000). A similar rule applies with regard to the treatment of the Alternative Minimum Tax exemption amount and the accumulated earnings tax credit.

REVIEW QUESTIONS

1. *How does the tax rate schedule applied to a controlled group of corporations differ from that applicable to separate unrelated corporations?*

   To prevent the splitting of income and the use of multiple exemptions for Alternative Minimum Tax and credits for accumulated earnings tax purposes the lower tax rates (15% and 25% at present) are to be applied by the controlled group as if it were a single corporation. Similar rules govern the use of the Alternative Minimum Tax exemption amount and the accumulated earnings tax credit.

2. *What types of controlled groups of corporations are there?*

   There exist two types of controlled groups of corporations. These are the parent-subsidiary controlled group and the brother-sister controlled group.

3. *What is Internal Revenue Code Section 482?*

   Internal Revenue Code Section 482 is a tax provision authorizing the Internal Revenue Service to reallocate items of income, deduction, and credit between related corporations in order to prevent tax evasion and more clearly reflect income.

4. *Are controlled groups of corporations required to file a consolidated return?*

   A consolidated return need not be filed by a controlled group unless each member of the group consents to doing so.

5. *Once elected, can the controlled group cease to file a consolidated return?*

   The controlled group can only terminate the filing of a consolidated return once validly elected with the consent of the Internal Revenue Service.

6. How does Internal Revenue Code Section 338 operate?

If the criteria of Section 338 are satisfied, the acquiring parent corporation may treat its acquisition of stock of the subsidiary corporation as the acquisition of the subsidiary's underlying assets. In implementing this treatment a special formula is prescribed pursuant to which a deemed sales price of the subsidiary's assets is determined. This sales price is then allocated to assets of the subsidiary in accordance with a prescribed hierarchy. Where allocation of an amount to an asset under the formula exceeds the adjusted basis of such asset the gain realized must be recognized.

CHAPTER 11

"S" CORPORATIONS

11.1   Passthrough

"S" corporations, are considered a passthrough entity. As a result, one of their main attributes is that income and loss flow through the "S" corporation and are reflected on its shareholders' tax returns.

11.2   Qualification Criteria

In order to qualify for and retain "S" corporation status certain requisites must be satisfied. These requisites include:

1) The corporation must be incorporated and organized within the United States (a domestic corporation).

2) The corporation must not be an ineligible corporation. Corporations considered ineligible include: banks, insurance companies, companies incorporated in U.S. possessions including Puerto Rico, and generally members of an affiliated group.

3) The corporation cannot have more than 35 shareholders. In determining the number of shareholders, if an "S" corporation has stock held by a husband and wife, it is considered to be held by one shareholder so long as the couple is married.

4) The corporation can only have as its shareholders individuals, and certain trusts and estates.

5) The corporation cannot have a nonresident alien as a shareholder.

6) The corporation is only permitted to have one class of stock issued and outstanding. A special rule provides a safe harbor to insure that straight debt will not be classified as a second class of stock.

11.3   Election

In order to be treated as an "S" corporation not only must the previous criteria be satisfied, but an appropriate and timely election must be made. This election is made on a Form 2553 to which all shareholders who have held stock in the corporation as of the date of election (during the year of election) must consent.

To be effective for the taxable year in which the election is made, the election must be made by the 15th day of the third month following the beginning of the taxable year. Should the election be made after such date, the election will not be effective until the following year.

11.4   Loss of "S" Corporation Status

Once a corporation becomes an "S" corporation such status may be lost should the corporation fail to satisfy the "S" corporation qualifying criteria or take steps to revoke its status. In this regard, "S" status may be terminated upon:

1) An election to revoke by shareholders holding a majority of the "S" corporation stock.

2) A new shareholder with greater than 50% interest not consenting to "S" corporation status.

3) Acquisition of a subsidiary.

4) An "S" corporation which was previously a "C" corpora-

tion has excess passive activity income. Excess passive activity income exists for this purpose if the corporation has passive income greater than 25% of its gross receipts for three consecutive taxable years and was previously a regular "C" corporation which has accumulated earnings and profits.

11.5 Regaining of "S" Corporation Status

"S" status may be reelected after a five year waiting period following loss of status. Where the cause of failure to retain status is inadvertent, an earlier reelection may be made pursuant to the consent of the Service.

11.6 Procedural Rules

The "S" corporation is generally required to file a Form 1120S by the 15th day of the third month following the end of its taxable year. This form is more an information return than a tax return. Items appearing on Form 1120S are allocated to shareholders based upon their pro-rata interest in the corporation during the taxable year of the "S" corporation. The Form 1120S reflects a net income figure composed of items where the tax treatment of these items does not differ between taxpayers, and shows separately those items of significance, the treatment of which may differ between taxpayers.

Generally an "S" corporation is required to use a calendar taxable year. A fiscal taxable year is permitted in certain circumstances where:

1) It is the corporation's natural business year.

2) There exists a valid business reason for use of a fiscal taxable year.

3) The "S" corporation's use of a fiscal taxable year is grandfathered in under an appropriate rule.

11.7   Potential Taxation of "S" Corporations

In certain situation an "S" corporation may be subject to tax. These situations primarily concern "S" corporations which were previously regular "C" corporations and pertain to:

1) Built in gains.

2) Excess net passive investment income.

3) LIFO recapture to the extent of FIFO inventory valuation in excess of LIFO inventory valuation when converting from "C" corporation to "S" corporation status.

11.8   Distributions of Property

When an "S" corporation distributes property to its shareholders, the "S" corporation must recognize gain to the extent that the fair market value of the asset distributed exceeds its adjusted basis. This gain is however passed through to the "S" corporation shareholders.

11.9   Effect to Shareholders

In determining the effect to shareholders of an "S" corporation distribution, the following three accounts must be taken into consideration:

Accumulated Adjustments Account (AAA) — This account consists of the total undistributed net income of the "S" corporation for its post-1982 taxable years.

Previously Taxed Income (PTI) — This account includes income previously taxed under old law.

Accumulated Earnings and Profits — This account consists of accumulated earnings and profits from prior regular corporation taxable years.

The following hierarchy is applied in determining the characterization of an "S" corporation in distributions to its shareholders:

1) The distribution is tax-free up to the amount of the shareholder's basis in "S" corporation stock to the extent of the corporation's Accumulated Adjustments Account.

2) Any distribution is tax-free to the extent considered to come from previously taxed income.

3) Any excess distributed constitutes a dividend to the extent of the corporation's accumulated earnings and profits.

4) Any remaining excess constitutes a return of capital which goes first to the recovery of any remaining stock basis of the shareholder with any excess being capital gain.

11.10 Basis and Amount at Risk

"S" corporation shareholders are entitled to utilize passthrough losses up to the amount that they are both at risk and possess a basis in their "S" corporation investment. Where the basis or amount at risk is insufficient to absorb the full amount of a passthrough loss, the excess will be carried forward and be generally useable when the shareholder has a sufficient basis and amount at risk at year-end to absorb the excess. Note that in determining a shareholder's basis in "S" corporation stock, the shareholder cannot include a share of liabilities outstanding at the corporate level.

11.11 Fringe Benefits

"S" corporations are subject to special restrictions with regard to the nature and type of fringe benefits they can provide their shareholders. These restrictions particularly apply to shareholders with a greater than 2% interest in the "S" corporation.

REVIEW QUESTIONS

1. *What is meant by an "S" corporation being a passthrough entity?*

   By being a passthrough entity the "S" corporation is characterized by items of income, deduction, and credit not being directly taxed to the corporation, but instead being passed through to shareholders for tax treatment at the shareholder level.

2. *What is the original due date of an "S" corporation's tax return?*

   As a general rule the tax return of an "S" corporation is due on the 15th day of the third month following the end of the "S" corporation's taxable year.

3. *What is the maximum number of shareholders that an "S" corporation is allowed to have?*

   The "S" corporation is permitted to have a maximum number of 35 shareholders. The type of shareholders an "S" corporation is permitted to have is also subject to limitation. In computing the number of shareholders, if the corporation has stock held by a husband and wife, this is considered held by one shareholder so long as the couple is married.

4. *How long must an "S" corporation generally wait before it can elect "S" corporation again after such status has been terminated?*

   As a general rule the corporation must wait for a five year period before it can reelect "S" corporation status again. The major exception to this period arises where the termination was inadvertent and the Internal Revenue Service consents to an earlier election.

5. *To be effective for the first taxable year in which an "S" corporation election is made, the election must be made by what date?*

To be effective for the first taxable year in which the election is made, the corporation must make the election by the 15th day of the third month following the beginning of such taxable year.

6. *On what form is an "S" corporation election application made?*

An "S" corporation's election application is to be made on a Form 2553.

7. *What is the "S" corporation tax return form?*

An "S" corporation's tax return form is the 1120S.

8. *An "S" corporation distributes property with a basis of $10,000 to a shareholder. The corporation has an adjusted basis in the asset of $7,000. The shareholder in turn has a basis in his "S" corporation stock of $9,000. The shareholder's share of the corporation's AAA is $6,000 and the corporation has $2,000 in accumulated earnings and profits. What is the tax treatment of the shareholder on the distribution?*

As a result of the distribution, the shareholder will have a total return of capital of $8,000 as this equals the $6,000 Accumulated Adjustments Account (which does not exceed the shareholder's basis) plus $2,000 return of capital after taking into account $2,000 in dividends due to the accumulated earnings and profits and account. Thus, the distribution reduces the shareholder's basis by $8,000 and produces $2,000 in ordinary income dividend.

9. *What is the tax effect to the corporation of the distribution described in question 8 above?*

The distribution produces some $3,000 in gain recognized to the corporation ($10,000 fair market value of the asset distributed minus $7,000 adjusted basis). This $3,000 gain is passed through to the shareholders who in turn will reflect their share of the $3,000 gain on their tax returns and adjustment the basis of their "S" corporation stock accordingly.

REA's **Test Preps**
The Best in Test Preparation